PERFECT PERFECT

URE PICTURE PICTUR
ECT PERFECT PERFEC

PICTURE PICTURE P
PERFECT PERFECT P

URE PICTURE PICTUR
ECT PERFECT PERFE

DR. SHAPIRO'S

PICTURE PERFECT

WEIGHT LOSS

DESSERTS AND SNACKS

DR. SHAPIRO'S

PICTURE PERFECT

WEIGHT LOSS

DESSERTS AND SNACKS

Dr. Howard M. Shapiro

RUNNING PRESS

PHILADELPHIA • LONDON

A Running Press® Miniature Edition™

Text 2000 by Dr. Howard M. Shapiro
Photography © Kurt Wilson/Rodale Images and Lou Manna

Printed in China

Library of Congress Cataloging-in-Publication Number
00 135515

ISBN 0-7624-0983-5

This book may be ordered by mail from the publisher.
Please include $1.00 for postage and handling.
But try your bookstore first!

Running Press Book Publishers
125 South Twenty-second Street
Philadelphia, PA 19103-4399

Introduction

*F*ed up with diets?

You're not alone.

For nearly 20 years, I have specialized in weight control at my practice in mid-Manhattan.

I used to think New Yorkers were unique in their weight concerns. But of course they're not. Millions of people across America want to lose weight. And perhaps our biggest temptations are between-meal snacks and after-meal desserts.

Once you develop food

awareness for snacks and desserts, you'll never have to count calories or grams of fat or worry about enjoying an occasional treat. You don't have to deprive yourself at an ice cream parlor, a dinner party, a restaurant—or even when you're just sitting by the TV.

After Food Awareness Training, one look is all it takes to help you make delicious snack and dessert choices that are right for you. Weight loss becomes automatic because you react automatically.

I don't tell my patients what

they can't eat or shouldn't eat. Instead, I talk about the choices that they can make. I ask them to subscribe to a few principles that, I believe, are the essential components of successful weight loss.

Look—No Bad Foods!

• **Any reason for eating is okay.** If you crave food, go right ahead and have some. Just eat the healthiest, lowest-calorie foods you find satisfying.

• **There are no bad foods.** There are times when only the

high-fat, high calorie foods will do. You're not cheating if you eat them, but there are also many alternatives.

* **There are no correct portions.** Hunger varies from person to person. Even if you eat a whole pint of sorbet, your diet isn't a failure.

* **An eating plan needs to suit your tastes and lifestyle.** You can continue your normal activities without interruption as you continue to work toward losing weight.

* **You're never on a diet.** You're

participating in an ongoing process of learning to make satisfying food choices.

Why Deprivation Diets Don't Work

To lose weight successfully, you either have to decrease your caloric intake or increase the number of calories expended through exercise—preferably both. You have to accomplish calorie reduction without feeling deprived. Feeling deprived kicks you in the rear end—right in the direction of the nearest hot-fudge sundae or the local bakery.

People who are attempting to lose weight typically do not report feelings of deprivation; they bury them instead. They will say things like, "I had plenty. I didn't need to eat the brownie."; "I wasn't hungry."; or "I don't know why I did it."

If those phrases sound familiar, I can assure you that people who are deprived of food do need to eat. If you eat, it's because you're hungry.

The Control Issue

Contrary to conventional wisdom, control is not the sure path to weight loss. In fact, control is the enemy. It suggests that someone wants to eat a particular food but refuses to do it with a mighty effort of will.

This kind of control goes hand in hand with deprivation, which ultimately spells trouble. When you lose weight by exercising control you're likely to regain that weight again as soon as you "lose control."

You're Choosing,
Not Cheating

With Food Awareness Training, you're always choosing, never cheating.

Obviously, you can't have every dessert in the world and still lose weight. But you do have some choices. I recommend you substitute the lower-calorie foods when possible, but have the brownie or the roll every now and then.

That Bedtime Snack

Eating right before bedtime? Isn't that an invitation to obesity?

Evidently not. Several studies confirm that when you eat has no connection with weight, and a survey by the Department of Agriculture has demonstrated that evening eating in particular has no more effect on your weight than morning eating.

It's the total number of calories consumed daily and expended in activity that makes—or breaks—weight gain.

Dr. Shapiro's Anytime Frozen Dessert List

Any nonfat yogurt or sorbet is good to have in your freezer. When selecting brands, be sure to keep an eye on the calories. Here are some that I like.

* In soft-serve, up to 25 calories per ounce, as in Columbo Lite
* In hard-pack, up to 450 calories per pint, as in Tofutti Light, and all brands of Italian ices
* In Creamsicles, frozen fudge bars, and popsicles, up to 45 calories per bar, as in Welch's Fruit

Juice Bars and chocolate mousse by Weight Watchers

* In individual packaged frozen bars, up to 100 calories each, as in FrozFruit.

But please, whatever you do, recognize that the decision is up to you. Making a conscious decision to enjoy something is very different from eating it and feeling like a failure. In the latter case, people often go on to an all-out binge, having decided that it doesn't matter since they've already blown the diet.

What's a Lot and What's Not

Unfortunately, most veteran dieters expect the acceptable foods to be something like lettuce leaves and celery stalks. We're suggesting food that you may decide to substitute for higher-calorie foods while getting the same satisfying taste.

Do you like chocolate ice cream? You can have the richest chocolate ice cream available—for about 1,350 calories a pint. But you have other choices. You can have chocolate frozen yogurt or sorbet—those have 450 calories a pint or less. If you think that a frozen fudge bar or two would be just as satisfying, you're really in luck, since a low-calorie fudge bar is only 30 calories. In other words, you'd have to eat 45 fudge bars to consume the same number of calories as you'd get from one pint of rich ice cream.

Hormones and Taste

Do your tastes change at different times of the month? For women, there's a hormonal reason why that happens.

Everybody knows that pregnant women are often seized by sudden tastes for salty or spicy food. The same thing happens premenstrually. Changing hormone levels affect the taste perception of salt, raising the salt taste threshold. Saltier, more savory, more highly flavored foods seem more appealing to women during these times.

Calories and Where They Come From

As you're making food choices, you will naturally lean towards foods that have lower calorie counts, since it's reasonable to assume that you want to lose weight. But in addition to this, I'd like to steer you toward foods that are high in nutritional value. It's another way to ensure that your needs are met when you're hungry. And, of course, it's a good way to make sure that you're getting all the vitamins, minerals, fiber, and protein that your body needs.

Nutrients are divided into two basic categories, macronutrients and micronutrients. Macronutrients are food substances like protein, fat, and carbohydrates that end up supplying us with calories.

A macronutrient has the potential to supply energy, and the actual production of energy is measured in calories. Calories are calculated by measuring the amount of heat a food gives off when it is "burned."

Micronutrients are food components like vitamins and minerals. These supply no calories, but they help release energy from food. So they're the sparks that help light the fire.

What about water? Technically, it doesn't fit in either category. It's not a macronutrient, because it has no calories. And it's not a micronutrient, because it's neither a vitamin nor a mineral.

But we all need water to live. It's absolutely essential for digestion as well as many other bodily processes.

Is Alcohol Fattening?

Drinking alcohol is a double whammy. Not only is booze high in calories, but it also evidently leads to increased appetite.

In a study, researchers alternated giving alcoholic and nonalcoholic aperitifs to a group of men and women lunchers over a 7-day period. When the group drank alcohol, they ate faster, ate more, ate for a longer time, became "full" later, and kept on eating after they had reached satiety.

Shopping Low-Calorie

Food labels are a great information source. They're the "study guide" to a lot of the foods that you're eating, and you'll find them on most food packages these days. This is information worth knowing. For example, by reading the Nutrition Facts label carefully, you can quickly learn how much of certain good guy nutrients like vitamins A and C, calcium, iron, and fiber the food contains. At a glance, you can compare those figures with the percentage Daily Value for such "bad guys" as saturated fat and cholesterol. If the label reveals that you're getting just 2 to 3 percent of the good guys while you're getting 20 to 30 percent of the bad guys, you know immediately you're on the wrong side of the tracks.

The Exercise Component

Every health professional in the country advises patients that exercise is important. Exercise helps prevent disease by strengthening your immune system. It makes you feel better, sleep better, work better. It improves your appearance. It raises your energy level. It even lifts your mood. And, proven beyond all doubt, exercise helps you lose and control weight.

Be Happy—Exercise!

Research studies confirm what people who exercise regularly have long suspected: Physical activity can actually make you happier. Some long-term studies suggest that physical fitness and the ability to be active may make people less likely to become depressed. It stands to reason: With exercise providing the benefits of weight control, high energy, and feeling good, who wouldn't be happier?

Research increasingly confirms that even short bouts of exercise, spaced intermittently throughout the day, enhance your overall fitness and contribute to weight control. A brisk walk up and down stairs, 10 minutes of lifting homemade weights, a quarter of an hour on the stationary bike all provide boosts to your system. And, say researchers, what counts is the total accumulation of exercise in a 24-hour period. In other words, whenever you exercise, it's beneficial.

The Write Stuff:
Your Own Food Diary

Now that you know that it's about making choices, it's time to begin keeping a food diary to see the choices you make. As you build awareness of your food habits and begin to see patterns in your eating, you will also begin to take more responsibility for your food choices.

Above all, you'll learn to be in touch with how you feel about food and about your eating habits. By forcing you to pay attention to the feelings you have about food and eating, the food diary makes you aware of your own ability to make choices. That's why it's your first step toward better choices—choices that will help you lose weight and keep it off through your lifetime.

How to Start:

Make 7 copies of the template you find on page 37. For a week, record every bite and sip you take—with the exception of water and low-calorie beverages.

Write down what you've had the minute you've eaten it—immediately. If you put off making the notation, you will almost certainly omit an important item in your entry.

Here's how to fill out each entry on the diary template.

• **Time.** Record the exact time that you are eating. Does the diary show that at certain times of the day you tend to eat more? Are other food choices available to you at those times?

• **Food.** Note what you have eaten, and how it was prepared, if applicable. Describe as many ingredients in the dish as you think necessary. What kind of choices do you make? Are you choosing mostly protein? Mostly starch? Or was it starch in the morning and protein in the afternoon?

* **Degree of Hunger.** For the purpose of this diary, define hunger as a desire to eat regardless of reason. Rate the desire on a scale from 0 to 4, with 0 indicating no hunger and 4 indicating extreme hunger. Does the diary show that you ate when you

didn't feel truly hungry? Sometimes? Often?

• **Situation (Place/Activity).** Where, and in what situation, were you when you had the food or drink? This information is helpful because I don't want you to change your lifestyle, just your relationship with food. Can you find any connection between the situation in which you found yourself and the fact that you reached for food? You may be able to see the connection between the situation and the kind of food you chose.

• **Comments.** Note anything you feel is relevant to your food choice or to the way you felt after eating. What do your comments tell you about your eating habits? What do they reveal about your hunger?

After you have scrupulously kept your food diary for a week sit down, look it over, and get ready to evaluate it.

You're looking for patterns— recurring situations in which you make food choices. The diary helps you see where you've chosen a high-calorie option or the less-healthy alternative.

Be honest and candid as you evaluate your food diary. Remember: This is an exercise in awareness. Nobody is asking you—now or ever—to change your eating habits or patterns in terms of when, why, or how you eat. The aim will be to find healthier, lower-calorie ways of working with those patterns. To get there, you must start with awareness.

The Food Diary

Time	Food (Preparation, Serving Size)	Degree of Hunger (0-4)	Situation (Place, Activity)	Comments

Snack Tricks

It isn't difficult to be deceived about snacks.

Those apple chips are not nearly the caloric bargain of that handful of pretzel rods. And for both nutrition and calorie-watching, nothing beats the real thing. Even if you ate four whole apples, you wouldn't be getting as many calories as you get from this 3-ounce serving of apple chips.

Equal Calories, Different Portions

3 oz apple chips 460 calories

4 medium apples 320 calories
4 pretzel rods 140 calories

TOTAL 460 calories

The Color Orange

Love cheese? Who doesn't? But its calorie content can make it a costly snack. The two bites of Cheddar on top are barely enough to satisfy a cheese craving, they contain as many calories as 30 dried apricot halves. And the apricots offer fiber and vitamin benefits too numerous to count.

Equal Calories, Different Portions

2 oz Cheddar cheese
240 calories

=

30 dried apricot halves
240 calories

Sweet Tooth
Bargain-Hunting

If it's sweet taste you crave, keep your options in mind. The sorbet bars and dried figs are equivalent in calorie count to the chocolate-covered ice cream bar.

1 Häagen-Dazs chocolate-covered ice cream bar 290 calories

Equal Calories, Different Portions

2 Häagen-Dazs chocolate sorbet bars 160 calories
6 small dried figs 130 calories

TOTAL 290 calories

Stacked Snack

In the mood for a rich snack? You can have one, two, or even more slices out of this stack of raisin bread generously slathered with low-sugar fruit spread. Even if you could eat the whole stack shown here, you'd just get the total number of calories that are contained in a single buttered scone.

1 scone (9 oz) **810** calories
1 Tbsp butter **120** calories

TOTAL 930 calories

=

14 slices raisin bread **840** calories
4 Tbsp low-sugar fruit spread **90** calories

TOTAL 930 calories

Crowded Out

If you think this one lonely scoop of rich chocolate chocolate-chip ice cream doesn't look like much, you're right. It isn't. For the same number of calories, you could eat 10 Tofutti chocolate fudge treats or 15 fresh, succulent plums.

Equal Calories, Different Portions

 = **½ cup rich chocolate-chip ice cream 300 calories**

=

10 Tofutti Chocolate Fudge Treats 300 calories

15 plums 300 calories

Lemon Aids

Sometimes, only the tart taste of lemon will do. One lemon tart can cost you as many calories as seven scoops of lemon sorbet or 14 lemon lollipops.

lemon pastry
420 calories

7 scoops lemon sorbet
420 calories

14 lemon lollipops
420 calories

Equal Calories, Different Portions

Spuds 'n Nuts

Both potatoes and nuts are nutritious, healthy foods. The difference is in how we eat them.

This single cup of cashew nuts costs 880 calories—the equivalent of eight baked potatoes with salsa!

1 cup of cashews
880 calories

Equal Calories, Different Portions

8 baked potatoes with salsa
880 calories

Measly Muesli

The tiny portion of muesli plus the three low-fat fruit slice candies have 310 calories. For the same 310 calories, you could eat four wedges of honeydew and four fruit leathers.

½ cup muesli **160** calories
1½ oz low-fat fruit slice candy **150** calories

TOTAL 310 calories

Equal Calories, Different Portions

4 fruit leathers 180 calories
4 honeydew wedges 130 calories

TOTAL 310 calories

Equal Calories, Different Portions

Nosh News

These pretzel nuggets are low-fat, salt-free, and contain oat bran. The fact is, even a little bowl of pretzel nuggets contains 800 calories. That's the exact number of calories represented by dried fruit, bananas, and four pretzel rods. The bananas and dried fruit are packed with fiber, vitamins, and minerals.

7 oz low-fat, no-salt, oat bran pretzel nuggets
800 calories

 =

Equal Calories, Different Portions

4 pretzel rods 140 calories
3 bananas 270 calories
5 dates 150 calories
6 prunes 150 calories
6 apricot halves 50 calories
6 dried apple rings 40 calories

TOTAL 800 calories

Mini Muffin, Maxi Impact

This tiny mini muffin has "only" 90 calories. These muffins usually come in packs of a dozen or 20. And they go down pretty fast.

Next time you think mini muffin, think yogurt cone instead. This frozen yogurt cone is a 90-calorie treat, the same as each muffin.

1 mini muffin (1 oz)
90 calories

Equal Calories, Different Portions

1 cone	20	calories
3½ oz frozen yogurt	70	calories
TOTAL	**90**	calories

Ice Cream in the Freezer

A lot of people can consume a pint of light ice cream in one sitting. That pint has as many calories as 32 low-cal Creamsicles. If you had one of these Creamsicles every day for an entire month, you'd consume the same number of calories found in that single pint of ice cream.

Equal Calories, Different Portions

1 pint light ice cream
800 calories

=

32 low-cal Creamsicles
800 calories

A Little Fruit

Want dessert? You'll pay 320 calories for a hint of apple in this small piece of apple crumb cake. But look at your choices. You can have the melon, mixed fruit, sorbet, and pastry taste of a biscotto for the same total calorie count.

apple crumb cake 320 calories

Equal Calories, Different Portions

½ honeydew melon **80** calories
mixed fruit **60** calories
4 oz sorbet **80** calories
biscotto **100** calories

TOTAL 320 calories

Equal Calories, Different Portions

An Apple a Day

If you're getting your apple intake in pie, it's costing you about 480 calories a wedge, the caloric equivalent of five baked apples.

1 wedge apple pie 480 calories

5 baked apples (made with cinnamon, ginger, and low-calorie sweetener) 480 **calories**

The Pastry Difference

Fruit tarts seem innocuous compared to desserts like cheesecake or chocolate layer cake.

In fact, that fruit tart is made with a pastry that's so high in fat and sugar that it takes 8 cups of fresh raspberries with whipped topping to equal a single raspberry tart.

1 raspberry tart
440 calories

8 cups raspberries with whipped topping
440 calories

Cookie Monster

Love cookies? The dessert bonanza pictured here—totaling up every last bite of fruit, frozen yogurt, and candy—has the same number of calories as this single, lonely black-and-white cookie.

1 black-and-white cookie (4¼ oz)
640 calories

Equal Calories, Different Portions

2 frozen yogurt cones **200** calories
large plate of fruit **200** calories
6 hard candies **120** calories
8 chocolate mint sticks **120** calories

TOTAL 640 calories

Fruit or Fruit Candy

Each of the fruits shown here has the calorie equivalent of the very small handful of low-fat candies beside it.

Keep in mind that the candies offer nothing in the way of nutrients. But each of these fruits is a treasure chest of vitamins, minerals, and fiber. And where the candies have many artificial flavorings that strive to give you fruit taste, the pineapple and melons are the real thing.

Equal Calories, Different Portions

2 oz gummy bears
200 calories

1 pineapple (2 lbs)
200 calories

Equal Calories, Different Portions

½ watermelon (4 lbs)
200 calories

=

2 oz fruit slice candy
200 calories

2 oz jelly beans 200 calories

=

**1 canary melon (3 lbs)
200 calories**

Pop Goes the Corn

How high in calories could a tiny handful of mixed nuts be?

Think again. Ten whole cups of popcorn are equivalent to one handful of the nuts.

2⅔ oz mixed nuts 400 calories

10 cups popcorn
400 calories

Buy by Weight

These three separate servings all weigh the same. So what's your best choice if you measure your selections in terms of calories?

The best choice is the dried fruit, but not bananas (which are fried) and pineapple (which is sugar-coated).

Equal Portions, Different Calories

6 oz pretzel nuggets
720 calories

6 oz banana chips and dried sweetened pineapple
720 calories

6 oz assorted dried fruit
420 calories

Equal Portions, Different Calories

Deception in Glass Dishes

Can you guess which of these seemingly "nutritionally correct" sweet snacks is the best calorie buy? Before you actually go out and buy these snacks, don't forget the numbers you see here.

1 cup yogurt raisins **1,120** calories

1 cup dried cranberries **760** calories

Equal Portions, Different Calories

1 cup low-fat granola 520 calories

1 cup raisins 640 calories

1 cup sugar-free jelly beans 720 calories

Saboteurs

How Sweet It Is

As for choosing between butterscotch candies and something as nutritious-looking as trail mix, you'd think, "No contest!"

For a little taste of Food Awareness Training, take a harder look. The candies are the caloric bargain: 32 of them are equivalent in calorie count to 4 oz. of trail mix.

4 oz trail mix
640 calories

=

32 butterscotch candies
640 calories

Twisted Saboteurs

A yogurt pretzel has just as much fat and just as many calories as a chocolate-covered pretzel. From the minute portion you see here, you'll get 140 calories. Try two pretzel rods and a total of four plums—you get the same number of calories as come from this small serving of yogurt pretzels.

1 oz yogurt pretzels
140 calories

2 pretzel rods 70 calories
4 plums 70 calories
TOTAL 140 calories

Saboteurs

Naturally Low-Calorie

This cup of Quaker Natural cereal has as many calories as 16 low-cal frozen fudge bars. So before you automatically reach for the "natural" product with its high calories, you'll probably want to consider what's underneath the equal sign.

1 cup Quarker Natural cereal
540 calories

=

16 low-fat frozen fudger bars 540 calories

Devilishly Angelic

True, you could eat this small slice of angel food cake with just a bit of raspberry sauce. But for the same calorie count, perhaps you'd rather help yourself to a huge bowl of mixed berries with whipped topping.

Saboteurs

1 slice angel food cake (3 oz) **300** calories
⅓ cup raspberry sauce **160** calories

TOTAL 460 calories

2 qt mixed berries
400 calories
large dollop whipped topping
60 calories

TOTAL 460 calories

The Pretzel Paradox

This soft pretzel is low in fat, but at 470 calories, it's no great weight-loss bargain. For about the same calorie count, you could have two 1 oz. packs of honey-roasted peanuts and 3 cups of fruit!

1 soft pretzel (6 oz)
470 calories

Hazardous Situations

2 containers fruit, 1½ cups each **120** calories
2 packs of peanuts, 1 oz each **350** calories

TOTAL 470 calories

"Coffee and . . ." at Starbucks

Just to remind you of your pastry choices in a typical Starbucks, look at the photo-message here. Keep in mind that the lemon pastry, which looks innocuous, isn't the lowest-calorie choice you can make.

lemon pastry
470 calories

low-fat muffin
230 calories

2 biscotti
180 calories

Holiday Meals

The Trick in the Treat

At 360 calories for this tiny portion, candy corn isn't much of a treat for the weight-conscious. 6 Tootsie Pops total the same number of calories. So, next Halloween, remember what else there is before you automatically reach for the candy corn.

3½ oz candy corn 360 calories

6 Tootsie Pops 360 calories

Holiday Meals

Be My Valentine

Almost criminally delicious, chocolate truffles are pretty much off the charts, calorie-wise. Consider offering just a taste or two of truffles and satisfying your beloved's chocolate craving with chocolate-dipped strawberries instead. And don't forget the rose—no calories at all!

8 truffles
(½ oz each)
560 calories

VS.

6 chocolate-dipped
strawberries **180** calories
2 truffles **140** calories

TOTAL 320 calories

Picture This:
The Weight is Over

Of course, I am not promising you that you will add years to your life, or that a funny and fabulous new personality will emerge. And I can't promise that you will become thinner than you've *ever* been when you change your relationship with food. What I am promising is that a changed relationship with food will add benefits to your life even as it subtracts pounds and takes away your fear of gaining weight.

Knowledge is power, as the saying goes, and the knowledge you gain from this book can give you the power you need to change the most constant, necessary, and ongoing relationship that you have—your relationship with food.

This book has been bound
using handcraft methods, and
Smyth-sewn to ensure durability.
The dust jacket and the interior
were designed by Terry Peterson.
The text was edited by
Victoria Hyun.
The text was set in Bembo,
Trade Gothic, and Bodoni.

PICTURE PICTURE PI
ERFECT PERFECT PE
E PICTURE PICTURE
T PERFECT PERFECT
ICTURE PICTURE PICT
ERFECT PERFECT PER
E PICTURE PICTURE
PERFECT PERFECT
ICTURE PICTURE PICT
ERFECT PERFECT PER